LIFESKILLS™ HANDBOOKS

Car *and Driver*

Emily Hutchinson

and

Susan M. Freese

21st CENTURY

SADDLEBACK
EDUCATIONAL PUBLISHING

SADDLEBACK
EDUCATIONAL PUBLISHING
www.sdlback.com

ISBN-13: 978-1-61651-688-8
ISBN-10: 1-61651-688-7
eBook: 978-1-61247-340-6

Printed in Guangzhou, China
1111/CA21101811

16 15 14 13 12   1 2 3 4 5

Contents

SECTION **1**

Becoming a Good Driver

Getting a driver's license is a huge step for most people! But becoming a good driver involves a lot more than just passing the driving test. To be well prepared, you should learn about handling a vehicle in bad weather and other hazardous conditions. You should also make sure you know how to use a map and what laws are in effect in your state.

What's Your Story?

Meet Diego

Diego is almost 16 years old, and he wants to learn how to drive. In the state where he used to live, he could already have had a license. He and his family lived in a rural area. The state allowed people there to begin driving when they're 14. But where Diego lives now, the laws are different. He can get a learner's permit when he's 15, but he can't get his license until

he's 16. Also, he must complete classroom and behind-the-wheel instruction taught by professionals.

Meet Kaylee

Kaylee is 18 years old. Like Diego, she wants to get a driver's license. But because she's an adult and lives in a different state, the laws for her are different. Kaylee doesn't

have to take professionally taught classroom or behind-the-wheel instruction. But she does have to get a learner's permit and practice driving before taking her test.

Meet Megan

Megan is 25 years old. She's lived most of her life in a big city. Like many people there, she has never had a driver's license. She's always counted on public transportation to get around. But in a few months, she will be moving to an area where things are really spread out and there are few buses. She will have to drive to work, to shop, and so on. The area is also well known for its bad weather—lots of rain and fog. Because of her age, Megan doesn't have to take driver training. But she thinks she will be a better driver if she does.

CHAPTER 1

Learning to Drive

Diego's Plan

Like most states, Diego's state has ***graduated licensing laws***. Those laws require him to get a learner's permit before being able to get a driver's license.

In Diego's state, getting a learner's permit requires taking a class in driver education. Diego's high school offers this class, so he's decided to sign up for it. In this one-semester course, he will learn the rules of the road and get some tips on safe driving. The class will prepare him for taking the written test needed to get a learner's permit.

Graduated Licensing Laws

Laws that provide different levels of privileges and restrictions for drivers. They are usually based on drivers' ages and levels of training and experience.

After Diego gets his learner's permit, he will be able to take behind-the-wheel training. For that, he will attend a driving school. A professional instructor will give Diego four 90-minute lessons.

Taking Your Driving Test

Visit the Web site of your state's Department of Motor Vehicles (DMV) to find out what to bring when you take your driving test. You might need to have any or all of the following:

- A completed driver's license application (signed by a parent or guardian, if you're under 18)
- Your learner's permit and proof of having completed training
- One or more valid forms of identification
- Payment for the license fee
- Proof of having auto insurance
- Your glasses or contact lenses (if needed to pass the vision test)
- A parent or guardian (if you're under 18)

To get a license in Diego's state, a driver under age 18 must complete 50 hours of supervised driving practice. Also, 10 of those hours must be at night. Diego's parents will help him complete the required time behind the wheel. Then, he will take his driving test at the local testing station.

Because Diego is under 18, his driver's license will be restricted. In his state, that means he won't be able to drive between 11:00 p.m. and 5:00 a.m. He also won't be able to have more than one passenger with him.

[FACT]

Restricted Licenses

Drivers under 18 usually have restrictions on the hours they can drive. Most states forbid teens to drive late at night and early in the morning. Exceptions are sometimes made when driving with an adult or when going to work or school. In addition, most states don't allow teen drivers to have more than one or two teenage passengers. This restriction usually applies for the first six months or more after getting a driver's license. Exceptions are sometimes made if an adult is present or the passengers are family members.

Risk Factors for Teen Drivers

Teens make up only 7% of all drivers, but they account for 14% of all car accident deaths. Why is this age group at such high risk for accidents?

- Don't often recognize hazards
- Bad at identifying risks
- Eager to take risks
- Don't always use seatbelts
- Have little driving skill and experience
- Tend to use alcohol and drugs
- Often have passengers
- Have little experience driving at night

Kaylee's Plan

To get her learner's permit, Kaylee will read the driver handbook and take the written test. After she has her permit, she will take behind-the-wheel training from her sister. By law, Kaylee can practice driving only with a person who is over age 25 and has a valid driver's license.

Kaylee's state doesn't require her to complete a certain number of hours of behind-the-wheel practice. Nor does the state require her to have a learner's permit for a certain length of time. She can take the driving test as soon as she feels ready. And because she's 18, her license will be unrestricted.

Underage Drinking and Driving

In many states, the penalties for getting a DUI (driving under the influence of alcohol) are harsher for drivers under 18 than for older drivers. For example, teen drivers often have their licenses automatically suspended for a year. They also face other penalties, such as fines and community service. Several states have also increased DUI penalties for drivers ages 18 to 21. These states want to enforce a zero-tolerance policy for underage drinking. (The legal drinking age is 21 in all states.) Penalties may include a license suspension and even the sale of the vehicle involved in the DUI.

Megan's Plan

Megan's state doesn't require her to take behind-the-wheel training from a professional instructor. She's worried, though, that she won't be able to pass the driving test unless she does. Getting professional instruction won't be cheap, based on the prices she's found. Even so, Megan thinks it will be worth it.

Finding a Driving School

Search online or in the phone book to find a professional driving school in your area. Most driving schools offer several kinds of programs. Some programs provide the minimum training required by the state. Others provide extra services, such as pick-up/drop-off and practice tests. Usually, the greater the number of services provided, the higher the cost of the program.

Before you sign up for a program, be sure to get in writing how much it costs. Also make sure you understand the number and length of sessions. Finally, make sure the school and its instructors have the licenses required by the state.

CHAPTER **2**

Getting a Driver's License

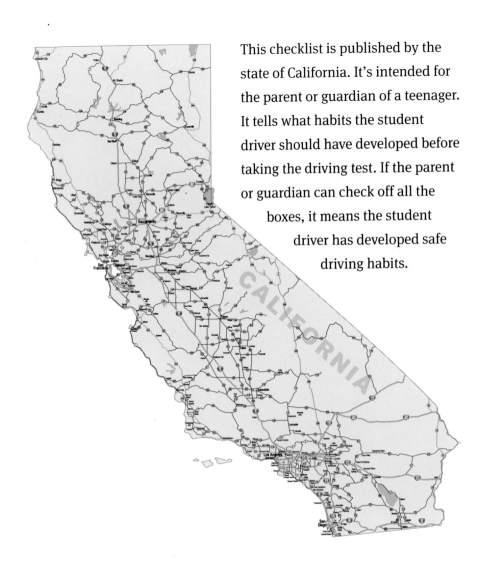

This checklist is published by the state of California. It's intended for the parent or guardian of a teenager. It tells what habits the student driver should have developed before taking the driving test. If the parent or guardian can check off all the boxes, it means the student driver has developed safe driving habits.

Locate the Controls

Your student driver knows where the following controls are located and how they work:

- ☐ Horn
- ☐ 4-way flashers
- ☐ Heater/defroster
- ☐ Windshield wipers
- ☐ Emergency and parking brakes
- ☐ Headlights

4-Way Flashers

The emergency or hazard lights located at the four corners of the vehicle. They are used to indicate the vehicle has stalled.

Before Starting the Vehicle

- ☐ Adjusts mirrors
- ☐ Fastens safety belt

Seat Belt Laws

Most states have laws requiring drivers and passengers to wear seat belts. In 18 states, a driver can be ticketed for a seat belt violation only when he or she has committed another traffic offense, such as speeding. But in 31 states, a driver can be stopped and ticketed solely for a seat belt violation. Some states also have special requirements for children. And some states require only front-seat passengers to be strapped in.

Starting the Vehicle

- ☐ Vehicle is in "Park" or "Neutral"
- ☐ Foot on brake
- ☐ Starts vehicle smoothly

Moving Forward

- ☐ Signals
- ☐ Looks over shoulder before pulling into traffic
- ☐ Uses both hands on opposite sides of steering wheel

Safe Hand Positions

For many years, drivers were told to hold the steering wheel at the "10 o'clock" and "2 o'clock" positions. Doing so was believed to provide the safest handling of the vehicle. But because vehicles today have air bags, holding the wheel at "10 and 2" may no longer be safe. If the driver's side air bag is set off, the force could break the driver's arms. It could also throw the driver's hands back against his or her face.

The American Automobile Association (AAA) recommends holding the steering wheel around "7 and 5" or "8 and 4." Many driving instructors and schools agree with this recommendation. However, other sources warn that injuries may still occur.

Stopping

- ☐ Stops when necessary behind crosswalk or limit line
- ☐ Uses correct foot on brake pedal

Stopping at Crosswalks

Some states have laws that require drivers to stop for pedestrians in crosswalks—not just slow down. Drivers must stop and stay stopped when a pedestrian is within one lane of their half of the roadway. Also, drivers that are turning must stop and stay stopped for a pedestrian in a crosswalk on the street around the corner.

Turns

- ☐ Signals and slows for turns
- ☐ Begins and ends turns in correct lane
- ☐ Yields **right-of-way** when necessary
- ☐ Accepts legal right-of-way when safe
- ☐ Sees and reacts to hazards

Right-of-Way

The legal right to cross a road first, before other drivers. In general, drivers on a main road have the right of way over drivers on a secondary road, such as a driveway. When two drivers arrive at an intersection at the same time, the driver on the right has the right of way.

Dangers of Backing Up

One of the most dangerous things drivers do every day is back up. Approximately one in four car accidents involves backing up. This comes to a total of more than 300,000 accidents a year in the United States.

Many of these accidents occur in driveways and parking lots. Sadly, they result in the injuries and deaths of young children. In a recent four-year period, 474 children were killed in backing-up accidents.

Backing Up

☐ Looks back over right shoulder when backing out the car

☐ Checks mirrors and glances quickly to side while backing up

Changing Lanes

☐ Signals

☐ Checks mirrors

☐ Checks over shoulder

☐ Changes lanes safely

Hill Parking

☐ Signals

☐ Curbs wheel properly

☐ Sets parking brake

☐ Signals and checks over shoulder before entering traffic

Parallel Parking

- ☐ Signals
- ☐ Looks over shoulder while backing
- ☐ Yields to other vehicles when necessary

Driving on the Freeway

- ☐ Checks traffic flow
- ☐ Signals
- ☐ Times entry onto freeway
- ☐ Checks over shoulder as he or she accelerates into gap in traffic
- ☐ Signals early and slows down on the exit ramp to posted speed limit
- ☐ Adjusts speed to road conditions

Defensive Driving Techniques

- ☐ Checks mirrors frequently and before braking
- ☐ Checks cross streets before entering intersections
- ☐ Checks signal lights and signs
- ☐ Keeps eyes "moving" (watches shoulders [sides] and middle of road)
- ☐ Keeps a "space cushion" around the car
- ☐ Follows at a safe distance

CHAPTER 3

Bad Weather and Other Hazards

Tips for Stopping Your Vehicle

If something is in your path, you need to see it in time to be able to stop. Assuming you have good tires, good brakes, and dry pavement, follow these guidelines for figuring out the *stopping distance*:

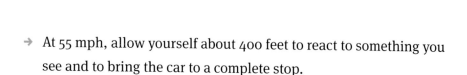

→ At 55 mph, allow yourself about 400 feet to react to something you see and to bring the car to a complete stop.

→ At 35 mph, allow yourself about 210 feet to react and to bring the car to a complete stop.

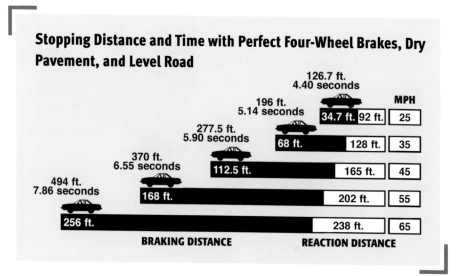

Stopping Distance and Time with Perfect Four-Wheel Brakes, Dry Pavement, and Level Road

Tips for Driving in Bad Weather

Adjust your driving to the weather and road conditions. That's the basic law for determining the safe speed to drive.

Also, turn on your lights during the day if it's hard to see. *But don't drive with only your parking lights on.*

Stopping Distance

How long it takes for a driver and vehicle to come to a complete stop. The shortest stopping distance is how long it takes the driver to react and then stop the vehicle.

Correct Use of Parking Lights

Parking lights are located outside the headlights on the front of a vehicle. Many vehicles also have parking lights in the back, outside the taillights. In emergencies, parking lights provide backup lighting. But by themselves, they don't provide enough light for driving at night. That's why it's illegal in most states to drive at night with only the parking lights on.

Fog

The best advice for driving in the fog is *don't*. Consider postponing your trip until the fog clears. If you must drive, however, follow these tips:

→ Slow down and turn on your low-beam headlights, not your high-beam headlights. The light from the high-beams will reflect back and cause glare. *Never drive with only your parking lights or fog lights turned on.*

→ Increase your **following distance**. Also, be prepared to stop within the space you can see in front of your vehicle. Avoid crossing or passing lanes of traffic unless it's absolutely necessary. Listen for traffic you can't see. For the best vision, use your wipers and defroster as necessary.

→ If the fog becomes so thick that you can barely see, pull *completely* off the road. Don't continue driving until you can see better. Also, turn off your lights. Otherwise, someone may see your taillights, think you're still on the road, and drive into you.

Following Distance

The distance at which one vehicle can safely follow another. The distance that's considered safe depends on the vehicle's speed and the weather, road, and traffic conditions.

Heavy Rain or Snow

In heavy rain or snow, you may not be able to see more than 100 feet ahead. When you can't see any farther than that, you can't safely drive faster than 30 mph. You may also have to stop from time to time to

How to Determine Following Distance

Follow what's called the *three-second rule* to make sure you're a safe distance from the vehicle in front of you:

1. Select a fixed object on or along the road ahead—for example, a sign, a tree, or an overpass.

2. Watch for when the vehicle ahead of you reaches that object. At that moment, count out three seconds: "One-one-thousand, two-one-thousand, three-one-thousand." If your vehicle reaches the object before you can count out three seconds, then you're following too closely.

The three-second rule applies during the day and with dry roads and low levels of traffic. Allow six seconds at night, in heavy traffic, and in light rain, snow, or fog. And give yourself nine seconds in very poor weather, such as heavy rain, snow, or fog.

wipe mud or snow off your windshield, headlights, and taillights. Also follow these guidelines:

→ Slow down at the first sign of rain, drizzle, or snow on the road. Many road surfaces are most slippery when they first get wet. That's because the oil and dust have not yet been washed away.

→ If you drive in a snowy area, carry tire chains. You can put them on if you suddenly find yourself in dangerous conditions. Make sure you have the correct number of

chains and that they fit your drive wheels. Also, learn how to put on the chains before you need to use them.

Using Snow Tires and Tire Chains

Laws about the use of snow tires and tire chains vary from one state to another. Some states restrict the use of snow tires and tire chains to certain times and places. For instance, they may be required from October 1 through May 1 in mountainous areas. Other states require the use of snow tires or tire chains to drive on routes consid-

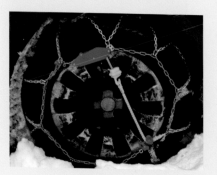

ered dangerous in winter. In Yosemite National Park, winter drivers are required by law to have tire chains with them. Also, some of the roads in the park are closed completely during the winter months.

Driving on Hills and Curves

Keep in mind that you never know what's on the other side of a steep hill or a sharp curve. So to be safe, slow down as you make the approach. That way, you'll have time to stop if a stalled vehicle or other object is blocking the road.

CHAPTER **4**

Using a City Map

Navigating with a Map

Diane was on her first trip to San
Francisco. She left her hotel on
foot with plans to visit her aunt.
Her aunt's address was in the 800
block of Lombard Street, between
Taylor and Jones Streets.

Diane took out a city map and
looked at the **street index**. She
found that Lombard Street was in Sections B-7, 9, and 10 on the map.
The part of the map shown on the next page includes Sections A and
B-9, 10, and 11. Using the map,
Diane found Lombard Street.

Next, Diane figured out where
she was on the map. That showed
her which way to go to reach
Lombard. She was at the corner
of Broadway and Stockton. From
there, she could take several
routes to get to Lombard Street.

Street Index

An alphabetical listing of
all the streets shown on the
map of a city. This index
also provides information
about what section of the
city each street appears in.

Diane's city map

Diane checked the *compass rose* and found that she would have to go north. But she didn't know which way was north. She walked one block and ended up on Pacific Street. By looking at the map, she could tell she was going the wrong way. So she backtracked, returning to Broadway. She crossed Broadway and walked up Stockton to Washington Square.

Compass Rose

The round or plus-shaped symbol on a map or compass that indicates the directions north, south, east, and west.

GPS (Global Positioning System)

A computerized navigation system. It uses a network of satellites to show the position of a vehicle.

"Just three more blocks to Lombard," Diane said to herself. Finally, she got to the corner of Stockton and Lombard. Another check of the map told her that she had to turn left to get to her aunt's apartment.

Navigating with GPS

Many new vehicles have **GPS (Global Positioning System)** equipment. So do a lot of smartphones and other devices. In most cases, typing in an address will provide a map and a set of directions for reaching your destination.

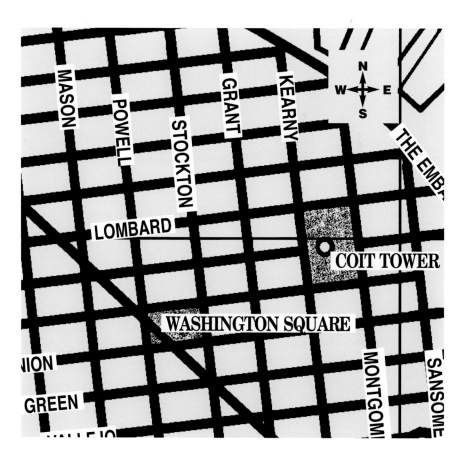

The maps required for a GPS navigation system are highly detailed. In addition to maps, the system stores information about streets and highways. This information might include speed limits, road names, and road numbers.

GPS maps are updated on a regular basis to show new roads. But not even the most current GPS maps are perfect. They may contain a

Free GPS

Like many new kinds of technology, the cost of GPS has gone down over the years. Even so, a new GPS device with the latest features can cost up to $1,000. But there are also free GPS tools available. You can download one onto your computer or phone and operate it from there.

The most widely available free GPS tool is Google Maps for Mobile. It provides both navigation and tracking, like other GPS devices. In addition, Google Maps has these helpful features:

- Audio (read-aloud) turn-by-turn directions
- Searching by address or type of business
- A street-view map, which lets you look at the surrounding area

few errors in addresses and street names, and some roads may even be missing. Even so, the routes mapped out by GPS are mostly accurate.

Many GPS devices can give you either the shortest route or the fastest route to your destination. Some can even calculate a new route in the case of a detour or heavy traffic.

GPS devices are also useful for *tracking*, or locating people. Many cell phones can be equipped with GPS tracking technology. Having this feature allows you to find the person who's carrying the phone. Even without this feature, someone who makes a 911 call from a cell phone can be located, too.

Navigating Safely

One advantage of using GPS is that you can usually choose to have the directions read aloud to you. If that's not an option with your GPS, then pull off the road to read the map or directions. The same goes for reading a regular map.

GPS and Driving Safety

Using GPS can make you a safer driver, for several reasons:
- You'll know where you're going, even in a new area.
- You won't have to handle a printed map while behind the wheel.
- When driving at night, you'll be told where to go without having to see street signs.
- You'll know which lane to be in before you have to make a turn.
- Depending on your GPS device, a call will be made to 911 or a repair service, if you need help.

Buying a Car

Buying a car is one of the biggest purchases you will ever make. And a lot more goes into that purchase than just picking out your dream vehicle! Setting a budget, deciding whether to buy new or used, and getting financing are all important steps in buying a car. With some careful planning, you can get the car that's right for you.

So You Want to Buy an SUV

Tony can hardly wait to have his own car! He's been thinking about what to buy for almost a year now.

At first, Tony was determined to buy his dream vehicle: a brand-new SUV with oversized tires and lots of accessories. But then reality set in. After visiting a couple of car dealerships, he realized that even a medium-sized

USED CARS & TRUCKS

SUV cost much more than he could afford. Plus, the costs of insuring and registering this kind of vehicle were both high. Buying gas would be expensive, too, because of the low mileage many SUVs get.

Next, Tony thought about buying an old used car—a "junker," his dad called it. He looked on CarSoup.com and found a couple of cars he could pay for outright. He'd been saving money for a while now. Tony liked the idea of not having a car payment. But he knew this kind of car would be expensive in terms of maintenance. A friend of his had bought an older car and was always having to fix something.

Tony has looked at a lot of cars and thought about all the financial issues. Now, he's ready to buy. He's decided on a small pickup that's five years old. It's not his dream vehicle. But it's one he can afford and will be able to count on for some years to come.

CHAPTER 1

Sticking to Your Budget

Stella had never had a brand-new car. And like Tony, she had a dream car in mind. Hers was a **hybrid** that got fantastic gas mileage and had lots of high-tech features.

When Stella visited the car dealership, she saw her dream car sitting in the lot. She could just see herself driving away in it! Then she looked at the sticker price, which appeared

Hybrid

A car that can run on two or more sources of energy. Usually, the energy sources are gas and electricity.

on the window of the car. Right away, she saw that it was 15% more than she wanted to pay.

Registration

Licensing a vehicle according to the terms required by the state in which it will be operated.

Stella had already determined the maximum price she could afford. If she went over it, she wouldn't be able to pay for gas, insurance, *registration*, maintenance, and other necessities. She really wanted a hybrid car. But every new model she looked at cost too much. She decided to look at other cars that got good gas mileage but had lower sticker prices.

Types of New Car Prices

Stella didn't realize that the sticker price is always negotiable. That means you can bargain with the car dealer to get a lower price. To bargain successfully, you should understand that there are three different prices of a new car:

1. **Sticker price:** The sticker price is based on the MSRP (Manufacturer's Suggested Retail Price). It allows the dealer to make a profit of anywhere from 7% to 25%, depending on the car. The average profit built in to an MSRP is 17% to 18%. In general, more expensive cars have higher *profit margins*.

2. **Dealer invoice:** The dealer invoice is the *wholesale price* of a new car. It's anywhere from 7% to 25% lower than the MSRP. For a midsize car, the dealer invoice is about 15% lower.

Profit Margins

The profit the dealer makes selling the car divided by what the dealer paid for the car. This amount is expressed as a percentage.

Wholesale Price

The reduced price charged to a customer who buys a large quantity of items. This customer usually intends to resell the items at a higher price.

3. **True invoice:** The true invoice is the price the dealer actually paid for the car. Sometimes, it's the same as the dealer invoice, but often, it's less. As a customer, you can't know this price for certain. One thing you can know for certain is that the true invoice is lower than the sticker price.

Online Resources

Check out these and other Web sites. They will give you information about the MSRPs and dealer invoices of all makes and models of new cars:

www.automobilemag.com
www.automotive.com
www.edmunds.com
www.internetautoguide.com
www.motortrend.com

What You *Should* Pay

Before visiting a car dealership, do some research. Find out the MSRP and dealer invoice on the model of the car you're interested in. Refer to Web sites such as Edmunds.com and books such as the *Autointelligence New Car Decision Maker*. Both provide the MSRP and dealer invoice for every vehicle and every option.

Also be prepared to negotiate with the dealer. Most people hate to do this, but it's an accepted part of the car-buying process. Keep in mind that you won't get what you want if you don't ask for it.

If you do your research and are a good negotiator, you shouldn't pay more than 3% over the dealer invoice. This amount represents both a fair price for you and a fair profit for the dealer.

Before giving up on her dream car, Stella did some research online, She learned the MSRP and dealer invoice for the hybrid she wanted. She also decided that she could bring down the price by giving up options like a sunroof, MP3 player adapter, GPS, and leather seats. By negotiating and offering just 3% over dealer invoice, she probably could afford the car of her dreams.

Negotiating Guidelines

- Before you begin negotiating, get as much information about the price and terms as you can.

- Don't negotiate with someone who intimidates you. Ask for another salesperson or go to another dealership.

- Take your time. Buying a car is a big decision.

- Eat before you go to the dealership. Don't let being hungry stop you from thinking clearly or make you rush into closing a deal.

- Be willing to take risks. Think like a salesperson, and look at negotiating as a game.

- Remember that you can walk away if you don't reach a deal that you like.

CHAPTER **2**

Comparing Used Cars

If money were no object, almost everyone would rather have a new car than a used one. But for most people, money is a big factor in deciding what car to buy.

The biggest concern over money is the high price of a new car. But another concern is that a new car loses much of its value the minute it's driven off the lot. In fact, the average new car loses 20% of its value within the first year and up to 65% within five years. This *depreciation* factor alone leads many people to look for used cars.

Depreciation
The drop in an item's value that occurs over time.

Places to Buy a Used Car

There are four places you can go to buy a used car:

1. **New-car dealers:** Many dealers sell both new and used cars. The used cars on their lots are usually late models that have been inspected. These cars often come with warranties and on-site service. Every car sold by a dealer must have a Buyers Guide label on the window. The buyer should scan the guide for information about the car's price and warranty. If the "As Is" box is checked, the car comes with no guarantees. If the "Warranty" box is checked, the buyer should read the information below the box. That information will tell what's covered.

Buyer's Guide Label

The Federal Trade Commission (FTC) requires car dealers to put a window sticker on every used car they sell. Called the *Buyers Guide*, that sticker must tell whether a warranty is offered. The dealer can provide an *express warranty*, which outlines the specific terms of

the guarantee. Or the dealer can sell the car *"as is,"* with no guarantee. The type of warranty and what it covers must be explained in the Buyers Guide.

[FACT]

New Car Prices

In 2010, the average price of a new car was $29,217. That price was up from $28,160 in 2009. What explains the price increase?

2009 **$28,160** 2010 **$29,217**

1. **Technology:** A package of options that includes a moonroof, stereo upgrade, and GPS adds about $3,000 to the price of the car. And about half that price goes to the dealer as profit.

2. **Buyer qualifications:** With today's tough economy, only people in excellent financial shape are buying new cars. These people tend to buy higher-quality and better-equipped cars. As a result, automakers are making models that fit those expectations.

Why New Cars Lose Their Value

Few items depreciate as quickly as a new car. But why?

- New cars become outdated. Different features and body styles come out every year.

- High-priced and stylish cars become outdated especially quickly. They also don't fit most people's needs and so aren't in great demand.

- Consumers often look down on cars made by less well known manufacturers. People don't think these cars hold their value as well as cars by more popular manufacturers and so the cars drop in value more quickly.

- Cars wear out. The average life expectancy of a car is only seven or eight years.

2. **Used-car dealers:** Buying a vehicle from a used-car dealer can be risky. These dealers' prices may be as much as 50% lower than those of new-car dealers. But they often sell vehicles that were rejected by reliable sellers. Sometimes, these cars have been in major accidents. If you decide to shop at a used-car lot, check out the dealer in advance. Make sure the owner has been in business for at least five years. Also check the owner's reputation with your state's Better Business Bureau.

Checking a Vehicle's Accident History

Before buying a used vehicle, find out whether it's ever been in an accident. You can do that using an online reporting system, such as Carfax.com or AutoCheck.com:

1. Before going online, locate the VIN *(Vehicle Identification Number)*. The easiest place to find the VIN is on a metal plate under the windshield on the driver's side.

2. At the Web site, enter the VIN number in the appropriate box. Then click on "Search."

3. When the report comes up, it will say whether the vehicle has been in an accident. It may also provide information about whether it's been in a flood and how many owners it's had.

VIN (Vehicle Identification Number)

The 17-digit serial number found on every passenger vehicle sold in the United States.

3. **Individuals:** Buying a used car from an individual is usually the cheapest way to go. The only problem is that individual sellers don't make any warranties. They might also fail to tell you everything you need to know about the car. Get as much information as you can by asking questions. Ask the seller about the car's condition. Ask whether it's ever been in an accident. Also ask about gas mileage and what kind of maintenance has been done. Then before you buy, have the car checked out by a mechanic you trust.

4. **Web sites:** Web sites such as AutoTrader.com, CarSoup.com, and CarsDirect.com provide links to new-car dealers in your area that sell used cars. To see what's available, enter your zip code and the make and model of the car you want. Also check out Web sites such as Craigslist and eBay. They have listings of used cars being sold by individuals.

Used-Car Checklist

When you go out looking at used cars, take a checklist with you. Look for answers to these questions:

- ☐ How many miles are on the car?
- ☐ Is the body in good condition?
- ☐ Is the interior in good condition?
- ☐ Has the car ever been in an accident?
- ☐ How worn are the tires?
- ☐ Is the tread wear on the tires uneven? (If so, there may be alignment problems.)

CHAPTER 3

Interpreting a New Car Sticker

When Dylan was at the car dealership, he looked at the window stickers on several cars he was interested in. Each sticker was posted on the front passenger-side window of the car and included the same basic information about the vehicle.

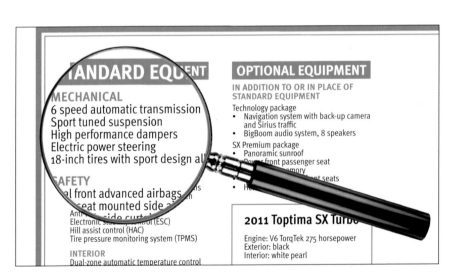

STANDARD EQUIPMENT

MECHANICAL
6 speed automatic transmission
Sport tuned suspension
High performance dampers
Electric power steering
18-inch tires with sport design al

SAFETY
al front advanced airbags
eat mounted side a
Anti ide curt
Electronic sta or (ESC)
Hill assist control (HAC)
Tire pressure monitoring system (TPMS)

INTERIOR
Dual-zone automatic temperature control

OPTIONAL EQUIPMENT

IN ADDITION TO OR IN PLACE OF
STANDARD EQUIPMENT
Technology package
• Navigation system with back-up camera
  and Sirius traffic
• BigBoom audio system, 8 speakers
SX Premium package
• Panoramic sunroof
• Po r front passenger seat
  emory
  t seats
• H

2011 Toptima SX Turbo

Engine: V6 TorqTek 275 horsepower
Exterior: black
Interior: white pearl

❶ Standard Equipment

Review this list of the basic features covered by the vehicle's MSRP (Manufacturer's Suggested Retail Price), or base price.

Order reference: 23244.23/1
Location: 8A232   Sales code E
Method of trans: truck   Port of entry: Port Hueneme

PARTS CONTENT content does not...
For vehicle...ution, or other non-parts co...2%
Major...
Fina...
...rdrolet of Los Angeles, Dealer number...
22 Mendota Avenue, Los Angeles, CA 900...

VIN
WP099AD34S356V554567S6671

Crash   Rear seat   ★★★★
Star ratings based on the risk of injury in a side impa...
Rollover   Rear seat   ★★★
Star ratings based on the risk of rollover in a single v...

ENVIRONMENTAL PER

Protect the environment, choose vehicles with hi...

Global Warming Score   **Smog Score**
7   5
1   10   1
Average   Average
new vehicle   new vehicle

② VIN (Vehicle Identification Number)

Check the VIN printed here against the number actually mounted on the car. Make sure they match. Also check the VIN on all the vehicle's paperwork.

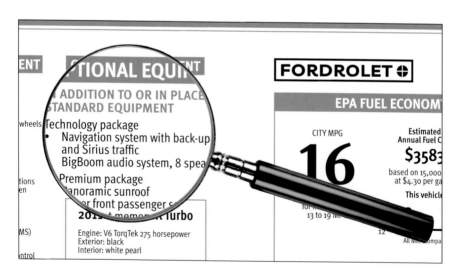

...TIONAL EQUI...
ADDITION TO OR IN PLACE
STANDARD EQUIPMENT

Technology package
• Navigation system with back-up
  and Sirius traffic
  BigBoom audio system, 8 spea...
Premium package
...anoramic sunroof
...r front passenger s...
201... ...Turbo
Engine: V6 TorqTek 275 horsepower
Exterior: black
Interior: white pearl

FORDROLET ⊕

EPA FUEL ECONOM

CITY MPG   Estimated
                        Annual Fuel C

16 $3583

                        based on 15,000
                        at $4.30 per ga

for...   This vehicle
13 to 19 M...

12

All m...compa...

③ Optional Equipment

Review this list of the optional features and what they cost. Note that these costs are added to the MSRP.

④ Total Suggested Retail Price

Check the Total Suggested Retail Price, often referred to as the "sticker price." It's the sum of all the costs stated on the sticker: the MSRP, charges for optional equipment, and the Destination and Delivery charge. The sticker price doesn't include taxes or fees related to the title and registration.

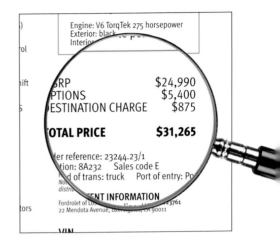

⑤ Mileage Estimates

Look at the MPG (miles per gallon) estimates provided for city and highway driving.

⑥ Safety Ratings

Examine the "star" ratings for front- and side-impact crashes and vehicle rollovers. (For more information about vehicle testing, go to www.safecar.gov.)

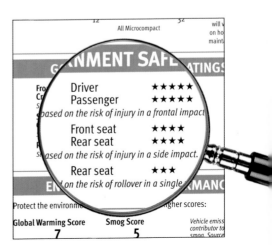

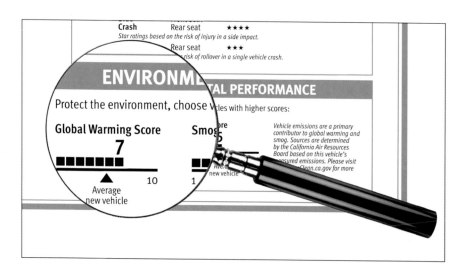

⑦ Emissions Information

See how the vehicle ranks in terms of smog emissions compared to other vehicles of the same model year.

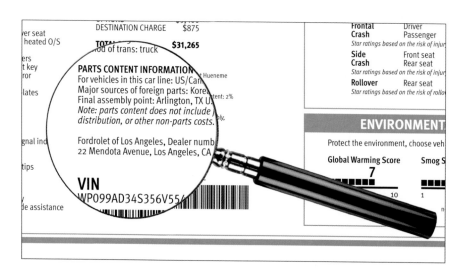

⑧ Assembly Information

Find out where the vehicle's major parts were made and where the vehicle was assembled.

① STANDARD EQUIPMENT

MECHANICAL
6 speed automatic transmission
Sport tuned suspension
High performance dampers
Electric power steering
18-inch tires with sport design alloy wheels

SAFETY
Dual front advanced airbags
Front seat mounted side airbags
Full-length side curtain airbags
Front active headrests
3-point seatbelts for all seating positions
Lower anchors and tethers for children
 (LATCH)
Anti-lock brake system (ABS)
Electronic stability control (ESC)
Hill assist control (HAC)
Tire pressure monitoring system (TPMS)

INTERIOR
Dual-zone automatic temperature control
AM/FM/CD/MP3 audio with 6 speakers
BLUETOOTH wireless technology
Leather and woven seat trim
Leather wrapped steering wheel and shift
 knob
8-way power adjustable driver seat
Power windows, door locks, heated O/S
 mirrors
Steering wheel paddle shifters
Push button start with smart key
Auto-dimming rear view mirror
Cruise control
Metal pedals and door sill plates
Floor mats

EXTERIOR
HID headlights
LED taillights
Outside mirrors with turn signal indicators
Front fog lights
Rear lip spoiler
Dual exhausts with chrome tips

WARRANTY
10 year / 100,000 mile
Limited powertrain warranty
5 year / 60,000 mile roadside assistance

③ OPTIONAL EQUIPMENT

**IN ADDITION TO OR IN PLACE OF
STANDARD EQUIPMENT**

Technology package
• Navigation system with back-up camera
 and Sirius traffic
• BigBoom audio system, 8 speakers

SX Premium package
• Panoramic sunroof
• Power front passenger seat
• Driver seat memory
• Heated and cooled front seats
• Heated outboard rear seats

2011 Toptima SX Turbo

Engine: V6 TorqTek 275 horsepower
Exterior: black
Interior: white pearl

MSRP | $24,990
OPTIONS | $5,400
DESTINATION CHARGE | $875

④ **TOTAL PRICE** | **$31,265**

Order reference: 23244.23/1
Location: 8A232   Sales code E
Method of trans: truck   Port of entry: Port Hueneme

⑧ **PARTS CONTENT INFORMATION**
For vehicles in this car line: US/Canada parts content: 2%
Major sources of foreign parts: Korea: 98%
Final assembly point: Arlington, TX U.S.A.
*Note: parts content does not include final assembly,
distribution, or other non-parts costs.*

Fordrolet of Los Angeles, Dealer number **0023761**
22 Mendota Avenue, Los Angeles, CA 90011

② **VIN**
WP099AD34S356V554567S66712

FORDROLET ⊕

EPA FUEL ECONOMY ESTIMATES

CITY MPG

⑤

16

Expected range
for most drivers
13 to 19 MPG

**Estimated
Annual Fuel Cost**

$3583

based on 15,000 miles
at $4.30 per gallon

This vehicle

18
▼

12 ———————— 32

All Microcompact

HIGHWAY MPG

23

Expected range
for most drivers
19 to 27 MPG

Your actual mileage
will vary depending
on how you drive and
maintain your vehicle.

GOVERNMENT SAFETY RATINGS

⑥

| **Frontal Crash** | Driver | ★★★★★ |
| | Passenger | ★★★★★ |

Star ratings based on the risk of injury in a frontal impact.

| **Side Crash** | Front seat | ★★★★ |
| | Rear seat | ★★★★ |

Star ratings based on the risk of injury in a side impact.

| **Rollover** | Rear seat | ★★★ |

Star ratings based on the risk of rollover in a single vehicle crash.

ENVIRONMENTAL PERFORMANCE

⑦ Protect the environment, choose vehicles with higher scores:

Global Warming Score

7

1   10
▲
Average
new vehicle

Smog Score

5

1   10
▲
Average
new vehicle

*Vehicle emissions are a primary
contributor to global warming and
smog. Sources are determined
by the California Air Resources
Board based on this vehicle's
measured emissions. Please visit
www.DriveClean.ca.gov for more
information.*

Financing a Car

Payment Options

The best way to buy a car is with cash. That way, you won't have to borrow money and pay interest. But most people don't have enough cash on hand and must borrow money. You should shop for a loan from several kinds of lenders, such as banks, credit unions, and finance companies.

Also get pre-approved for the loan. Then you'll know what you can afford and what limits are involved. Compare the **_APRs (Annual Percentage Rates)_** and other terms from different lenders to find the best deal.

APR (Annual Percentage Rate)

What you pay to borrow money each year for the entire term of the loan. It includes the annual interest rate plus any transaction fees.

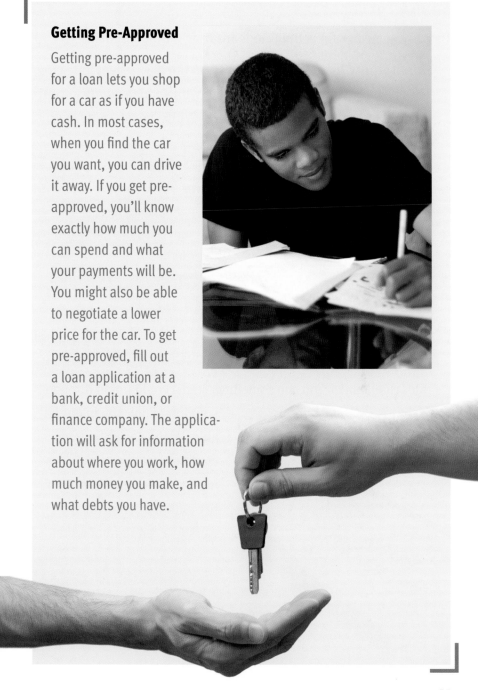

Getting Pre-Approved

Getting pre-approved for a loan lets you shop for a car as if you have cash. In most cases, when you find the car you want, you can drive it away. If you get pre-approved, you'll know exactly how much you can spend and what your payments will be. You might also be able to negotiate a lower price for the car. To get pre-approved, fill out a loan application at a bank, credit union, or finance company. The application will ask for information about where you work, how much money you make, and what debts you have.

Sources of Car Loans

Here are some tips for getting car loans from different sources:

→ **Home equity loan:** A home equity loan offers excellent financing. To get one, you must be a homeowner with enough *equity* in your home to finance the amount you need. With a home equity loan, you can deduct the interest payments on your tax return. With a conventional auto loan from another kind of lender, you cannot deduct the interest.

Equity

The amount of value or owner-ship you have in something. It's determined by subtracting what you owe on the item from what the item is worth.

→ **Credit union:** If you belong to a credit union, check its loan rates. Credit unions often have lower interest rates than banks. You can sometimes join a credit union through your job. If not, you might be able to join a neighborhood credit union. Some credit unions accept members who live within a certain area or work in a certain profession.

8.5% 10.75%
9.25%
10.9% 7.5%
12% 6.25%

→ **Banks and finance companies:** Do you have a checking account or a credit card account with a bank? If so, that's a good place to get a car loan. But check interest rates at several banks before you make a commitment. Check with finance companies, too. Their interest rates will probably be higher than those at banks. But they may be more willing to give you a loan, especially if you have a low credit rating.

Your Credit Rating

One of the things lenders check in deciding whether to give you a loan is your credit rating. That rating is based on reports from banks, credit card companies, and others about how much debt you have and whether you pay your bills on time. Your credit rating is like your financial report card. When you apply for a loan, most lenders check your FICO score. It's a number ranging from 300 to 850. The higher the number, the better your credit rating.

→ **Dealer financing:** Some car dealers offer loans on their own. Their interest rates aren't usually the best you can get, but sometimes they are. Customers with excellent credit may get a low interest rate. It's a good idea to see what the dealership is offering before you make a final decision.

Down Payment

How much of your own money you put toward the cost of something at the time of purchase.

Most banks and finance companies expect you to make a **down payment** of 20%. This means that you must pay 20% of the car's cost up front and on your own. Your loan will be for the other 80% and paid off over time. If you can put down more than 20%, you should. The bigger the down payment you make, the smaller the loan you'll need. And the smaller the loan, the lower your monthly payment will be.

Leasing

Leasing is an option for some people. A lease is a type of vehicle rental agreement. It often doesn't require a down payment, but it still requires having good credit. A lease may have restrictions, such as limited miles and required maintenance. It might also have a penalty if you need to get out of the lease before it expires. Plus, at the end of a lease, you won't have any equity in the vehicle to put toward a new car.

Calculating Your Car Payment

Suppose you want to buy a car that costs $25,000. You're trying to decide how much money to put down and how much to borrow. You've been pre-approved for a loan of up to $20,000. The interest rate on the loan is 10%, and the term is five years. Look  at how much the amount of your down payment affects your monthly payment and the total you pay for the car:

Down Payment	Loan Amount	Monthly Payment	Total Interest Paid	Total Paid on Loan	Total Paid for Car
$5,000	$20,000	$424.94	$5,496.45	$25,496.45	$30,496.45
$6,000	$19,000	$403.69	$5,221.63	$24,221.63	$30,221.63
$7,000	$18,000	$382.45	$4,946.81	$22,946.81	$29,946.81
$8,000	$17,000	$361.20	$4,671.99	$21,671.99	$29,671.99
$9,000	$16,000	$339.95	$4,397.16	$20,397.16	$29,397.16
$10,000	$15,000	$318.71	$4,122.34	$19,122.34	$29,122.34

SECTION 3

Maintenance and Repair

Few things are as frustrating as having your car break down! Breaking down can be dangerous, too, depending on when and where it happens. You can keep your car on the road by doing regular maintenance. And if by chance it does break down, you can save time and money by knowing how best to make the needed repairs.

When's the Last Time You Checked Your Spare Tire?

Wednesday was a busy day for Nina. She had class most of the morning and then had to be at work at noon. Most days, driving there took only 15 or 20 minutes. But today, it was snowing. She would have to allow extra time.

Nina hurried out to her car and discovered immediately that she had a problem: The car had a flat tire. She quickly set about changing it. She was sure she could do the job herself. After all, she had changed a flat last summer—or maybe the summer before.

Nina dug around inside the trunk, looking for the jack and wrench. Where could they be? They were supposed to be stored in a case and clamped to the side of the trunk. Nina dug under the floor of the trunk, where the spare tire was kept. She found the jack and wrench. They were lying loose next to the tire.

Nina took out the jack and wrench and laid them on the ground. Then she pulled out the spare tire and leaned it against the side of the car. Something about the tire didn't seem right.

Nina pushed on the tire with her foot and realized it was quite soft. It didn't have enough air in it! How could that be? When was the last time she had checked the spare? Not recently, she thought.

Disgusted, Nina took her phone out of her pocket and called work. She was going to be late, she said—really late.

CHAPTER **1**

Benefits of Upkeep

Car experts offer a lot of specific tips for taking care of your car. But one thing they all agree on is the importance of doing regular maintenance.

Read Your Owner's Manual

The best source of information about car maintenance is your owner's manual. Read through it after you buy your car.

If you didn't get the owner's manual with your car, you should buy it. Call the local dealership that sells your type of car. It will be able to get you the manual if your car is fairly new. If your car is older, try ordering the manual online. You might also try a junkyard.

The owner's manual provides information about what kinds of maintenance to do and how often. You will probably not be able to do most of this work yourself, but you can learn how to check things, such oil and radiator fluid levels. And you can learn how often to bring your car into the shop for service.

Nina's Plan for Car Maintenance

Nina's experience with the flat tire made her determined to take good care of her car. If she didn't do regular maintenance, she knew she would risk getting stranded. She also knew that she would end up paying costly repair bills. So, she worked up the plan on pages 66–67.

Action	How Often?	Why?
Change the oil.	Every 3,000 miles or every three months, whichever comes first.	Engines operate better with clean oil.
Change the oil filter.	Every time the oil is changed.	A dirty filter will have dirty oil in it. That oil will get mixed in with the fresh oil.
Check the **boots** over all the joints.	Every time the oil is changed.	If the boots are torn or cracked, dirt will get in and the grease around the joints will escape. Without grease, the metal in the joints of the steering and suspension system will not move smoothly.
Change the air filter.	Usually, every six months.	The air filter makes sure that clean air goes into the **combustion chambers** of the cylinders. If it's dirty, they won't work correctly.

Car Maintenance

Action	How Often?	Why?
Check the following fluids: **coolant,** windshield washer, transmission, and power steering.	Once a month.	If these fluids get low, the car won't operate as well. It may also become unsafe and have expensive damage.
Clean the front and rear lights.	Whenever they get dirty.	Lights are essential to seeing and being seen at night.
Clean all the windows and the windshield wiper blades.	Whenever they get dirty.	For safety, it's important to be able to see out the windows.
Check the air pressure in the tires.	Once a month.	Tires will wear out faster if the air pressure isn't correct.
Rotate the tires.	Every 5,000 to 10,000 miles.	Rotating the tires will help ensure even tread wear.

Checking Air Pressure

Keeping your tires inflated at the recommended pressure will make them last longer. It will also help you get better gas mileage and give you a smoother ride. You can find the air pressure recommended for your tires in the owner's manual. It's also usually printed on a sticker posted inside the door on the driver's side. For most passenger cars, the recommended pressure is 32 psi (pounds per square inch). To get an accurate reading, check the tires when they're cold. Tires are more inflated when warm and less inflated when cold.

Boots

Protective coverings that attach to the CV (constant velocity) joints on the vehicle's drive shaft. They hold the grease in place.

Combustion Chamber

The part of the engine where the mixture of air and fuel is compressed by the piston and ignited by the spark plug. This process produces energy and moves the vehicle.

Coolant

The colored fluid (usually green or red) that's mixed with water in the radiator. It's sometimes called *antifreeze*, because it keeps the water from freezing in the winter and boiling over in the summer. The coolant also lubricates parts of the engine.

Tips for Rotating Tires

- Rotate the tires front to rear, but keep them on the same side. If your spare is a regular tire, work it into the rotation.

- Check the owner's manual to determine how often to rotate the tires. Or follow the general rule of rotating the tires every 5,000 to 10,000 miles.

- Stay on a regular rotation schedule. For instance, rotate your tires every second or third time you change your oil.

- Pay attention to how the car handles when braking and when the road is wet or icy. If you have difficulty, you may need to rotate or replace the tires.

Importance of Changing the Oil

Think of your car's oil as its lifeblood. Changing the oil regularly may be the most important thing you do to keep your car running well. Check your owner's manual to find out how often to change the oil. Also find out what kind of oil and how much to use. Most manufacturers recommend changing the oil every three months or every 3,000 miles.

CHAPTER 2

Car Repair Estimates

Car parts wear out, and different parts last different lengths of time. Regular maintenance will help make sure parts last as long as possible. But sooner or later, something is bound to break down.

If you drive an older vehicle, you may feel like you're always making repairs. Three months ago, you had your brakes redone. Then your transmission needed some work. After you paid for that, you needed a new alternator. The repairs are never ending, it seems.

Mechanical Repairs

What should you do when your car sounds funny, acts strangely, or won't start? Here are some suggestions:

→ Take the car or have it towed to a garage or repair shop. Have the mechanic figure out the problem and give you a written *estimate* of the cost to fix it. If you think the estimate sounds too high, go somewhere else and get another estimate. You will have to pay the first mechanic for the time it took to figure out the problem. But you won't have to leave the car there to be fixed.

→ Get a few more estimates. Then compare them both in terms of cost and what work is going to be done. Estimates from car dealers are usually higher than those from garages and repair shops. But remember that the mechanics at car dealers are used to working on the same kinds of cars. They may also have better access to necessary parts and equipment. For these reasons, some people think car dealers' mechanics do better work. However, other people think car dealers' mechanics overcharge.

Estimate

The approximate cost of making the repairs. It's usually presented in a detailed list of parts and labor and their costs.

Car Repair Tips

- Regular repairs and maintenance can be done at just about any full-service repair shop. But have problems with a specific system, such as the transmission, done at a shop that specializes in that kind of work.

- Make an appointment to bring in your vehicle. At that time, give a general description of the problem. Doing that may help ensure the right kind of mechanic is on hand when you bring your car in.

- When you talk to the mechanic, describe the problem as best you can. But don't suggest what needs to be repaired or replaced. Let the mechanic decide what work is needed.

- Read the repair order before signing it or agreeing to have work done. Watch out for general statements, such as "Fix transmission." Don't ever sign a blank repair order or tell a mechanic to "do what's necessary."

Accident Repairs

What if your car is in an accident? Here are some guidelines for getting it fixed:

→ If the damage is great, report the accident to your car insurance company. Depending on your **coverage,** your insurance company may pay for some of the repairs. The insurance company will usually ask you to get at least three estimates.

→ If the damage is minor, you might not want to report it to your insurance company. Some insurance companies will drop you if you make too many **claims.** If there's limited damage, you might want to pay for the repairs yourself—especially if your collision **deductible** is high. In any case, follow the same steps as you would for a regular repair. Take the car to at least three repair shops. Compare the prices, but remember that price isn't the only thing to think about.

Coverage
The kinds of insurance a driver has and the levels of payouts they provide.

Claim
A request for payment based on the coverage provided by an insurance policy.

Deductible
The dollar amount someone who's insured must pay to repair or replace a damaged vehicle before the insurance company pays anything.

Also ask these questions: Does the shop have a good reputation? Does it seem efficient? Do you trust the mechanics? Base your decision on both price and the reputation of the shop. And if you don't know anything about the shop's reputation, check with your state's Better Business Bureau.

[FACT]

Report or Don't Report?

How do you know whether to report a car accident to your insurance company? Consider the cost of the repairs against the amount of your deductible. For example, suppose you have a $500 deductible:

- If the repairs cost $500 or less, you'll have to pay for everything. There's no reason to report the accident.

- If the repairs cost $650, you'll have to pay for almost everything. You might want to pay the entire cost and avoid making an insurance claim.

- If the repairs cost $2,000, you'll have to pay for just 25%. You should definitely report the accident.

CHAPTER 3

Using Jumper Cables

Jacob and Nathan met at the local movie theater. Each arrived separately in his own car. When they came out of the theater several hours later, Jacob realized he had accidentally left his car lights on. The car wouldn't start, and it sounded like the battery was dead.

"Great! A dead battery!" Jacob muttered to himself. "Now what?"

Jacob was just about ready to call the *auto club* for a tow when he had a brilliant idea. He had some *jumper cables* in his trunk. Maybe Nathan could give him a jump start.

"Hey, Nathan!" Jacob called out across the parking lot. "My

battery's dead. How about a jump?"

"No problem, Jacob," said Nathan. "Let me bring my car over."

Within 20 minutes, the two friends were back on the road.

Auto Club

A service that provides roadside assistance and other benefits to individuals with paid memberships. One example is the American Automobile Association (AAA).

Jumper Cables

A pair of long, thick, insulated electrical cables with large clamps on the ends. Jumper cables are used to start a stalled vehicle by connecting its dead battery to the live battery of another vehicle.

Causes of a Dead Battery

- **Leaving the lights on:** Leaving on the headlights or the interior lights is the most common cause of a dead battery. Many vehicles have bells or buzzers that go off when the headlights have been left on or a door hasn't been shut.

- **Low battery charge:** The battery can slowly run down in a vehicle that's not driven for a long time. Jump starting will likely get the vehicle going. But it must be driven or left running to recharge the battery.

- **Old age:** The average car battery lasts just three to five years. Then it needs to be replaced. Jump starting an old battery may get the vehicle going, but the battery won't hold a charge for long.

Steps for Jump Starting a Vehicle

1. Position the two cars so they are lined up hood to hood. This will mean parking the running vehicle next to the stalled vehicle or in front of and facing the stalled vehicle. Try to get the two cars' batteries as close to one another as possible.

2. Make sure each vehicle is in "Park," and put on its emergency brake. Also shut off the ignition in each car, along with the lights, radio, air conditioning, and other accessories.

3. Locate the ends of the red (positive) jumper cable. Then locate the positive terminal of each car's battery (the one with the "plus" sign on it). Clip the positive ends of the cable to the positive terminals of the batteries.

4. Locate the ends of the black (negative) jumper cable. Clip one end to the negative terminal (the one with the "minus" sign) on the running vehicle's battery. Clip the other end to a clean, unpainted metal (but not aluminum) surface in the engine compartment of the stalled vehicle, such as a bolt or a bracket. Choose a location that's as far away from the battery as possible.

5. Start the engine of the running vehicle. Let it run for 2 or 3 minutes.

6. Turn on the ignition in the stalled vehicle. After it starts, turn off the engine in the working vehicle. Its battery is no longer needed. Keep the newly started vehicle running for 30 minutes or so to recharge the battery.

[FACT]

Grounding the Vehicle

Why do you attach the black (negative) cable to an unpainted metal surface in the stalled car? Doing so allows the electrical current to ground out. Grounding uses the earth as a return path for the electricity.

7. To disconnect the cables, follow the reverse order in which you connected them:

   (1) Remove the black (negative) cable from the newly started vehicle.

   (2) Remove the black (negative) cable from the running vehicle.

   (3) Remove the red (positive) cable from the newly started vehicle.

   (4) Remove the red (positive) cable from the running vehicle.

Safety Guidelines for Jump Starting

- Before attaching the cables, check the stalled vehicle's battery. Look for cracks, corrosion, and loose or exposed wires. If the battery shows any of these problems, don't go ahead with the jump start.

- Make sure both vehicles have been placed in "Park." Also make sure their ignitions have been shut off.

- Connect the cables to the batteries in the proper order.

- Don't allow the ends of the jumper cables to touch.

- Wear safety goggles.

- Stand back as much as possible from the engine compartment. Also keep bystanders clear.

- Don't allow anyone to smoke around either vehicle.

What If Jump Starting Doesn't Work?

- On the stalled car, adjust how the red (positive) cable is connected to the battery. Try reclamping it or turning it slightly to get a better connection. Also brush off both vehicles' battery terminals to ensure a good connection is being made.

- Rev up the engine of the running vehicle, or let it run awhile longer to warm up.

- On the stalled vehicle, check that all accessories have been shut off. Also make sure all the doors have been completely shut.

- Try a different set of jumper cables or even a different vehicle. Jump starting works best if the two vehicles are about the same size or the running vehicle is larger than the stalled vehicle.

CHAPTER 4

New Tire Warranty

When Justina bought new tires from Steady Eddie's Tire Company Store, she read the ***warranty.*** She found the language hard to understand, though. She wanted to make sure she knew what problems with the tires would and wouldn't be covered. So, she rewrote the warranty in language that was easier to understand. See how much you understand in reading the original warranty and Justina's rewritten warranty.

Warranty

A written guarantee about the quality of a product made by the manufacturer. It usually includes steps for fixing or replacing the product if there's a problem.

The Original Warranty

For a fee collected at the time of the original tire purchase, Steady Eddie's Tire Company Store or affiliated Dandy Dan's Tire Stores will refund the purchase price and the sales tax, if any, on any tire in the event of a failure due to ***workmanship and materials*** or a non-

Workmanship and Materials

The quality of the skill or labor used to make something and the elements used to make it.

> **Tread**
>
> The part of the tire that touches the road. The band of rubber and grooves that runs all the way around the tire.

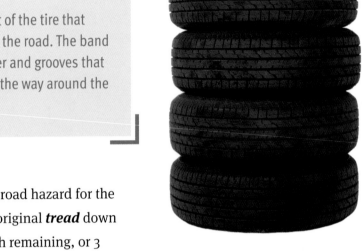

repairable road hazard for the life of the original **tread** down to 3/32 inch remaining, or 3 years from date of purchase, whichever occurs first. At the election of the purchaser, we will sell a replacement tire to the purchaser at the same price paid for the damaged tire, plus the required sales tax. In the event the original tire is discontinued or not available, a tire of similar value will be substituted.

If, in our opinion, the tire can be safely repaired, we will do so free of charge. The cost of this warranty is set forth on the receipt issued for the purchase of tire(s).

This warranty will be honored at any Steady Eddie's Tire Company Store or affiliated Dandy Dan's Tire Stores. This warranty does not cover damage caused by collision, vandalism, chain damage, mechanical defects of the vehicle, or willful abuse.

There will be additional charges to purchase a warranty for a replacement tire and to balance a replacement tire.

Valid only with purchase and presentation of warranty.

Justina's Rewritten Warranty

If you pay us extra money when you buy the tire, we will give you a warranty. The warranty says that if the tire fails because it was poorly made or was made from faulty materials, we will return your money. If the original tread is less than 3/32 of an inch, however, we will not refund your money. If you've had the tire for three years, we will not refund your money. If you like, we will sell you another tire for the same price as the damaged tire. If we don't have a tire just like the original one, we'll sell you one that's worth the same.

If we think we can repair the tire, we will do so at no cost. To find out how much this warranty costs, look at your receipt.

This warranty will be honored by us or by our partners. If the tire was damaged in a crash, by vandals, or by the use of chains, we won't refund your money. If the tire was damaged because something is wrong with your car, we won't refund your money. If you did something to the tire on purpose, we won't refund your money.

You will have to pay extra for a warranty on the new tire. You will also have to pay to get the new tire balanced.

To get your money back, you must buy this warranty and show it to us when you come in with a problem.

Checking Your Tire Tread

1. **Look at the wear bars:** Most tires today have wear bars, which look like small bumps in the grooves of the tire. Wear bars are exactly 2/32 inch high. When the tread is higher than the wear bars, the tire has enough tread to be driven on. But when the tread is level with the wear bars, the tire is worn out and should be replaced.

2. **Use a penny:** Insert a penny into one of the grooves in the tread with Lincoln's head turned down, into the tread. The tire has enough tread as long as part of the head is covered when the coin is inserted into the tread. But if the top of the head is visible, the tire is worn and should be replaced.

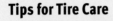

Tips for Tire Care

- **Pressure:** Keep your tires inflated at the proper air pressure. For most car tires, 32 psi (pounds per square inch) is recommended.

- **Alignment:** If your car tends to veer off in a particular direction, its wheels are likely out of alignment. Have the wheels aligned at a tire dealer or auto repair shop.

- **Rotation:** Rotate your tires every 5,000 to 10,000 miles. And at every rotation, check the wear on the tire tread to ensure it's mostly even on all four tires.

- **Tread:** Measure the tread on your tires on a regular basis, and pay attention to differences in wear. Uneven tread wear may mean your wheels need to be aligned or your tires need to be balanced.

Balanced Tires

Many tires are lighter or heavier on different sides, which means they aren't perfectly balanced. When mounted on your car, an unbalanced tire may wobble. It may also make your car pull to the side when you apply the brakes. Both of these problems tend to make the tire wear unevenly and need to be replaced sooner than it should. Driving with unbalanced tires also lowers your gas mileage. It may even damage your car's axles.

When you buy new tires, make sure they are tested for balance and corrected as needed. A tire can be balanced by having wheel weights placed on the lighter side.

Driving and the Law

Driving is considered a privilege, not a right. That means to drive legally, you must obey the laws of the state in which you live. Following those laws will prevent you from facing a range of penalties, from getting a ticket to losing your driver's license. Following driving laws will also keep you safe while you're out on the road.

Going Out on Your Own

Pat had a busy week ahead of him. On Saturday, he was graduating from college after five years of hard work. And on Thursday, he was moving out of his apartment and heading across the state to take a new job.

Sometime during the week, Pat also had to deal with buying and selling cars. He was selling the old car his parents had let him drive during college. He was also buying a new car from a local dealer. He knew the dealer would take care of registering his new car with the state. But his parents had to do the paperwork to turn over his old car to the new owner. They actually owned the car, so this was their responsibility. To help out, Pat went online to the Web site of the state's Department of Motor Vehicles (DMV). There, he found directions for what to do, along with the required forms.

Also, for the first time in his life, Pat had to arrange for his own car insurance. While he was a student and driving his parents' car, he'd been covered by their policy. But now, he'd be on his own. He was worried that the speeding ticket he'd received last year would mean higher insurance payments. Hopefully, graduating from college and getting a full-time job would reduce the impact of the ticket. Pat had talked to several insurance agents. He planned on looking carefully at their cost estimates before agreeing to a policy.

CHAPTER **1**

Automobile Registration

Why Register Your Vehicle?

When you register your vehicle, you're showing that you own it. You're also paying a fee to the government for the right to drive it—usually, to the state. That fee is paid annually and covers several kinds of costs, such as building and maintaining roads. Registration also allows the government to enforce certain requirements for owning and driving a vehicle. For instance, drivers may be required to have valid auto insurance and to make sure their cars meet standards for air pollution emissions.

Registering a Vehicle in California

Michael lives in California, and he wants to register the car he just bought. To learn how, he found some information in the *California Driver Handbook*. He also found some information online at the Web site of California's Department of Motor Vehicles (DMV) (www.dmv.ca.gov). In particular, he found the Notice of Transfer and Release of Liability form on page 97 and other forms he needed.

Fees and Licenses

The fee that's paid to register a vehicle is often based on the vehicle's value. The more expensive the vehicle, the higher the fee. Different types of vehicles also pay different fees, usually according to weight and use. For instance, commercial vehicles, such as buses and trucks, pay higher fees than cars intended for personal use.

When you register your vehicle, you get a license plate. It's sometimes referred to as *tags* or *tabs*. Most states require having one or two license plates mounted on the car. Of course, driving a vehicle requires having a valid driver's license. The registration covers the licensing of the vehicle, not the driver.

Getting Registration Forms

Get the registration forms you need from your state's Department of Motor Vehicles (DMV):

1. **Online:** Visit the DMV's Web site, and search for the term "Registration." Identify the forms you need, and print them out or download them to your computer.

2. **In person:** Visit the DMV or a branch office to get the forms you need. Also talk to someone there if you have questions about how to register your vehicle.

3. **By telephone:** Ask someone in the DMV's customer service department to help you determine which forms you need and send them to you by mail.

Buying from a Car Dealer

When you purchase a new or used vehicle from a licensed car dealer in California, the dealer collects sales tax and fees to register and title the vehicle. The dealer submits the fees and documents to the DMV and gives you a temporary operating authority. Usually, within six to eight weeks after you buy the car, you receive a registration card, stickers, and a **certificate of title**, if appropriate.

Certificate of Title

An official document that establishes proof of who owns a vehicle. It identifies the vehicle's year, make, and model; its VIN (Vehicle Identification Number); and its mileage at the time of the last sale. The title also provides the name and address of the owner and anyone else who has an ownership interest in the vehicle (called a *lien holder*), such as a bank.

Buying from a Private Party

If you purchase a vehicle from a private party, you are responsible for officially transferring the ownership within 10 days. To do so, submit these items:

→ A properly endorsed and completed certificate of title or application for duplicate title (REG 227)

→ The smog certification, if required, which should be provided by the seller

→ The use tax payment, if required

→ The **odometer disclosure statement**, if applicable

→ All appropriate DMV fees

Odometer Disclosure Statement

An official record of a vehicle's mileage at the time it's sold. This record may be provided on a special form or stated on the certificate of title.

Selling or Transferring

When you sell or **transfer** a vehicle, report it to DMV within 5 days on the Notice of Release of Liability form (REG 138). Enter the name and address of the purchaser and the date you sold or transferred the vehicle. Complete the entire form.

Transferring

The process in which the owner of a vehicle reassigns ownership to another person. This usually occurs following the sale of the vehicle.

Transferring Ownership and Liability

When you sell a vehicle and transfer ownership, you're also transferring liability for the vehicle to the new owner. If you don't complete the transfer within the required time period, you will likely remain responsible for any tickets or accidents involving the vehicle. Check with your state to see what's required. You may have to complete a special form to be released from liability. Then, you may have to send or bring in the form to the DMV or another agency to have the information recorded.

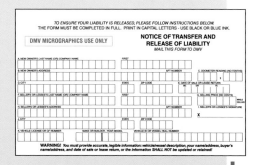

CHAPTER 2

Shopping for Car Insurance

To drive legally, you must have the car insurance that's required by your state. Most states have **minimum** insurance requirements, especially for **liability**. However, the levels of coverage required vary widely from state to state. And because of these differences,

the premiums paid for car insurance also vary widely across states.

The penalty for failing to meet insurance requirements also varies from state to state. In some states, you will be charged a large fine, and in others, you will lose your driver's license. To find out the minimum requirements for your state, contact the state insurance commissioner's office.

Minimum

The least or smallest amount that's possible or allowed.

Liability

Legal responsibility for injury or damage that has occurred.

Types of Car Insurance

A car insurance policy may have these kinds of coverage:

1. **Collision insurance** pays for the repair or replacement of your car if it's damaged in an accident that was your fault.

2. **Comprehensive insurance** pays for damage caused by theft, fire, hail, and other damage to your car.

3. **Liability insurance** covers injuries, medical costs, and damages to other people and their property. Liability is sometimes divided into two categories: personal injury and property damage.

4. **Uninsured motorist insurance** pays to repair your car if you get hit by someone with no insurance.

5. **No-fault insurance** covers only the driver's injuries and car damage. Under the no-fault system, it isn't necessary to determine whose fault the accident was.

The premiums you pay will depend on which kinds of insurance you have and what dollar amounts will be paid out in the case of a claim. The greater your level of coverage, the higher your premiums. Your premiums will also be affected by the level of risk you pose as a driver. That will be determined by your insurance company. Drivers who have accidents and get speeding tickets are considered at high risk and pay higher premiums.

Are You Considered a High-Risk Driver?

Your insurance company may consider you a high-risk driver if you have any of these qualities:

- Have had a DUI or DWI in the last 5 to 10 years
- Have had your license suspended or taken away in the last 5 years
- Have had a moving violation in the last 3 or 4 years
- Have been at fault in an accident in the last 4 years
- Have been penalized with fines or points in the last 4 years
- Have a bad credit rating or no credit history
- Are single or divorced
- Have only a high school diploma or GED (no college)
- Use your vehicle commercially
- Are in a high-risk occupation

Getting the Most for Your Money

To reduce the premiums you pay for car insurance, follow these guide-lines:

1. **Shop around.** Go online or make phone calls. Find and compare premiums at several insurance companies and agencies. But don't consider only price in choosing a company or agent. Service counts, too. Find out how the company and the agent handle claims before you make your choice.

2. **Ask about *discounts*.** An insurance agent can tell you how you might lower the premiums you pay. For example, having a higher deductible will give you a lower premium. ***Enrolling*** in a driver training course might lower your premium, too. Likewise, earning good grades and having a good driving record might help. Some companies give discounts for having airbags, anti-lock brakes, and car alarms.

3. **Limit your coverage.** If your car is worth less than $1,000, you might decide not to buy collision and/or comprehensive coverage. It might be less expensive to replace the car than insure it.

4. **Buy the right car.** Some cars cost more to insure because they are popular

Enroll
To register for or agree to take part in something.

Discount
A cut or reduction in the regular price. Car insurance discounts are usually offered to low-risk drivers.

with car thieves. Others have high premiums because they cost a lot to repair after an accident. Before you buy a car, find out how much the annual insurance premiums will be.

Deciding on the Right Amount of Coverage

You don't want to pay for more insurance coverage than you need. But you do want to make sure you have enough coverage to protect yourself financially in the case of an accident. Having only the minimum coverage required by your state might result in your getting sued. For example, suppose your state requires you to have $20,000 of coverage for property damage. That means your insurance company will pay $20,000 per accident to cover damage to other people's vehicles and property. But if fixing the damage costs more than that, someone might sue you to recover the full amount.

CHAPTER 3

Traffic and Parking Tickets

If you get a traffic ticket or a parking ticket, you can pay it or you can fight it. If you believe you are innocent, you can fight the ticket by appearing in court and explaining your case. If you are successful, you might get the charge dismissed or reduced.

Whatever you do, *don't ignore the ticket*. That will only lead to more problems. You can lose your license if you ignore tickets.

Handling a Traffic Ticket

Dealing with a ticket can be confusing, but each state has well-established rules about what to do. Check with your state's DMV to find out. Be respectful, but don't be shy about asking questions.

This is how the state of California's driver handbook explains its process for violations involving drivers believed to be *negligent.*

Negligent

In California, the term used to describe drivers who "fail to use the degree of care expected to avoid accidents." Expectations include "driving defensively, considering traffic, road and weather conditions, familiarity with the road, the type and conditions of their vehicles, level of driving skill and by maintaining control of their vehicles."

Negligent Driving and Loss of License for Adults

If you are stopped by a police officer and cited for a traffic law violation, you sign a promise to appear in traffic court. Before you go to court, you may have to pay *bail*, whether you are guilty or not, to ensure that you will show up. When you go to court, you may plead guilty or not guilty, or you may *forfeit* (pay) bail if you haven't already done so. Forfeiting bail is the same as a guilty plea. You may also have to pay additional fines.

If you ignore the traffic ticket, and don't keep your promise to appear in court, the failure to appear (FTA) goes on your driver record. If you fail to pay a fine (FTP), the Department of Motor Vehicles will state this on your driver record. Even one FTA or FTP can cause the department to *suspend* your license. Ending the suspension will cost you a reissue fee of $55.

Bail

The money paid to release someone from jail and to ensure he or she will appear in court.

Suspend

To take away someone's driver's license for a period of time, usually up to two years. Suspension is different from *revocation*, which involves a longer or permanent loss of a driver's license.

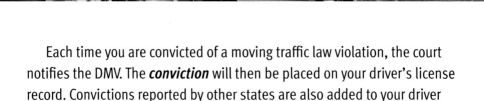

Each time you are convicted of a moving traffic law violation, the court notifies the DMV. The **_conviction_** will then be placed on your driver's license record. Convictions reported by other states are also added to your driver record.

Point Systems for Traffic Violations

In many states, drivers are given points for traffic violations. In general, serious offenses have higher point values than minor offenses. For example, driving 20 miles an hour over the speed limit might be worth four points. But not coming to a complete stop at a stop sign might be worth two points. The state's DMV keeps track of all drivers' points. Reaching a certain point total or earning a lot of points in a certain time period will result in penalties. In many cases, the driver's license is suspended or revoked. Drivers that rack up points also pay higher car insurance premiums.

Conviction
To have been found guilty of a crime, as charged.

Points on a Driver Record

The department keeps a public record of all your traffic convictions and accidents. Each occurrence stays on your record for 36 months or longer, depending on the type of conviction.

When might you be considered a negligent operator of a motor vehicle? When your driving record shows any one of the following "point count" totals, regardless of your *license class:*

License Class

The kind of driver's license someone has. Different classes of licenses are based on the weights of vehicles and their intended uses. Most states distinguish between commercial and noncommercial classes of licenses.

- 4 points in 12 months
- 6 points in 24 months
- 8 points in 36 months

Examples of one-point violations:

- A traffic conviction
- An at-fault accident

Examples of two-point violations:

- Reckless driving
- Driving under the influence of alcohol/drugs (DUI)
- Hit-and-run driving
- Evading a peace officer
- Driving while suspended or revoked
- Driving on the wrong side of the road

  If you get too many "points," you will lose your driver's license.

CHAPTER **4**

Dangerous Driving Habits

Each state has laws forbidding individuals from doing certain things while driving. For instance, each state has laws against drunk driving. They may be referred to as laws against DUI (Driving Under the Influence), DWI (Driving While Intoxicated), or OUI (Operating Under the Influence). These laws prohibit individuals from driving when they have consumed enough alcohol to reach an unsafe **BAC (Blood Alcohol Concentration).** In most states, that level is 0.08% for drivers of noncommercial vehicles who are of legal drinking age. The BAC is lower for both commercial drivers and drivers under 21 (the legal drinking age).

In recent years, some states have also put in place laws prohibiting behaviors that distract people while driving. Those behaviors include

BAC (Blood Alcohol Concentration)

The amount of alcohol in someone's bloodstream, indicated in percent. This may also be called *BAL (Blood Alcohol Level).*

using hand-held phones and text messaging. Some experts say these so-called ***distracted driving*** habits are as dangerous as drunk driving. Increased reports of accidents caused by distracted drivers have drawn attention to these behaviors and how to control them.

To learn about the current driving laws in your state, check the state's driver handbook or DMV Web site.

Distracted Driving

As defined by the US Department of Transportation, "any non-driving activity a person engages in that has the potential to distract him or her from the primary task of driving and increase the risk of crashing."

DUIs for Commercial Vehicle Drivers

In 1986, the US government put in place a series of standards to
ensure that individuals with CDLs (Commercial Drivers' Licenses)
are qualified and safe drivers. One of those standards set the BAC
for commercial drivers at 0.04%—half the BAC for noncommercial
drivers. For someone with a CDL, driving a commercial vehicle with
a 0.04% BAC is a major offense and could result in losing his or her
license. Driving a noncommercial vehicle with a 0.08% BAC and
refusing to take a BAC test are also major offenses and could result in
a loss of license.

Determining Alcohol Impairment

The box below was prepared by the California DMV and several other government agencies. It explains how the state of California defines alcohol *impairment*. In addition, the chart at the bottom of the box shows how many drinks it takes to reach different BAC levels. Note that many factors influence how alcohol affects someone, including his or her weight and the timeframe during which he or she drinks.

Impairment

A loss of or abnormality in physical or mental functioning.

ALCOHOL IMPAIRMENT CHART
DRIVING UNDER THE INFLUENCE OF
ALCOHOL AND/OR DRUGS IS ILLEGAL

Prepared by DMV in cooperation with the CHP, Office of Traffic Safety, Department of Alcohol and Drug Programs, and Department of Justice.

There is no safe way to drive while under the influence (DUI). Even one drink can make you an unsafe driver. Drinking affects your **BLOOD ALCOHOL CONCENTRATION** (**BAC**). It is illegal to drive in the U.S. with a **BAC** of .08% or more (.04% or more if you drive commercial vehicles or .01% or more if under 21). Even a **BAC** below .08% does not mean that it is safe or legal to drive.

For more on how different levels of BAC affect your body and driving ability, see www.stopimpaired driving.org/ABCsBACWeb/page2.htm

The chart below shows the **BAC** zones for various numbers of drinks and time periods.

HOW TO USE THESE CHARTS: Find the chart that includes your weight. Look at the total number of drinks you have had and compare that to the time shown. You can quickly tell if you are at risk of being arrested.* If your **BAC** level is in the gray zone, your chances of having an accident are 5 times

than if you had no drinks, and 25 times higher if your BAC level falls into the black zone.

REMEMBER: One drink is a 1¼-ounce shot of 80-proof liquor (even if it's mixed with non-alcoholic drinks), a 4-ounce glass of wine, or 10 ounces of 5.7% beer. If you have larger or stronger drinks, drink on an empty stomach, are tired, sick, upset, or have taken medicines or rugs, you can be **UNSAFE WITH FEWER DRINKS**.

TECHNICAL NOTE: These charts are guides and are not legal evidence of the actual **BAC**. Although it is possible for anyone to exceed the designated limits, the charts have been constructed so that fewer than 5 persons in 100 will exceed these limits when drinking the stated amounts on an empty stomach. Actual values can vary by body type, sex, health status, and other factors.

*VC 23152, VC 23153, VC 23135, VC 23140 DUI/Driving under the influence of alcohol and/or other drugs.

BAC Zones	90 to 109 lbs.	110 to 129 lbs.	130 to 149 lbs.	150 to 169 lbs.	170 to 189 lbs	190 to 209 lbs	210 lbs. & Up
TIME from 1st drink	TOTAL DRINKS 1 2 3 4 5 6 7 8	TOTAL DRINKS 1 2 3 4 5 6 7 8	TOTAL DRINKS 1 2 3 4 5 6 7 8	TOTAL DRINKS 1 2 3 4 5 6 7 8	TOTAL DRINKS 1 2 3 4 5 6 7 8	TOTAL DRINKS 1 2 3 4 5 6 7 8	TOTAL DRINKS 1 2 3 4 5 6 7 8
1 HR							
2 HRS							
3 HRS							
4 HRS							

CHART SHADINGS MEAN:
☐ .01%–.04% MAY BE DUI—DEFINITELY UNLAWFUL IF UNDER 21 YRS. OLD**
▨ .05%–.07% LIKELY DUI—DEFINITELY UNLAWFUL IF UNDER 21 YRS. OLD
■ .08% Up DEFINITELY DUI

****NOTE:** It is unlawful for anyone under 21 years of age to drive with a BAC of .01% or higher.
If caught driving with a .01% BAC or higher, the driving privilege is lost for one year.

Types of Distracted Driving

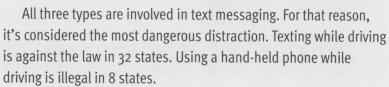

1. **Visual:** Taking your eyes off the road

2. **Manual:** Taking your hands off the wheel

3. **Cognitive:** Taking your mind off what you're doing

All three types are involved in text messaging. For that reason, it's considered the most dangerous distraction. Texting while driving is against the law in 32 states. Using a hand-held phone while driving is illegal in 8 states.

[FACT]

The Dangers of Distracted Driving

- In 2009, 20% of injury accidents involved distracted driving.

- Almost 5,500 people were killed, and another 448,000 were injured.

- Of the people killed, 995 died in accidents involving cell phone use.

- In the under-20 age group, 16% of the drivers involved in fatal accidents were distracted while driving.

- Drivers that use hand-held devices are four times as likely as other drivers to have a car accident serious enough to cause injury.

- Using a cell phone while driving delays a driver's reaction time as much as having a BAC of 0.08%. This is true whether the phone is held or used hands free.

Word List

abnormal
abuse
accelerate
access
accessories
accident
accurate
adjust
afford
agent
alcohol
alignment
alphabetical
annually
application
appointment
appropriate
approximately
assembly
assistance
assume
audio
automatically

bail
battery
behavior
budget
bystanders

calculate
checklist
claim
cognitive
collision
commercial
commitment

compartment
complicated
comprehensive
compress
computerize
confuse
conventional
conviction
corrosion
costly
coverage
crosswalk

damage
dangerous
dealership
deduct
deductible
defect
depreciation
destination
detailed
detour
device
disclosure
discontinued
discount
disgusted
dismiss
distracted
document
download
duplicate

economy
efficient
emergency

endorse
enforce
engage
enroll
ensure
equity
essential
estimate
examine
exception
expectation
expensive
expert
expire
expose

factor
familiarity
faulty
financial
fixed
fluid
forbid
forfeit
freeway
frustrating
fuel
full-service
functioning

graduated
guarantee
guardian
guidelines

handling
harsh

hazard
high-tech
honored
hybrid

ignore
impact
impairment
income
indicate
inflated
injury
innocent
insert
inspection
instruction
insulated
insure
interest
interior
interpret
intersection
intimidate
intoxicated
invoice

jump-start
junkyard

lease
lender
liability
licensing
limited
loan
lubricate

Word List

maintenance
mapped
material
maximum
mechanical
mileage
minimum
minor
mountainous
mutter

navigate
necessity
negative
negligent
negotiate
network
noncommercial
nonrepairable

occurrence
odometer
offense
on-site
online
option
outdated
outright
overcharge
overpass
oversized
ownership

paperwork
particular
passenger
pavement

payout
pedestrian
penalty
percent
permanent
plea
policy
postpone
potential
pre-approve
premium
presentation
pressure
primary
privilege
professional
profit
prohibit
protective

qualifications
qualified

rating
reaction
reality
realize
reassign
receipt
recharge
recommend
recover
refund
register
registration
reject
reliable

replacement
reputation
request
resell
residential
resource
responsibility
restriction
reverse
revoke
rewritten
right-of-way
rotate
route
routine

satellite
scan
schedule
secondary
section
signal
slippery
smog
source
specialize
stalled
statement
stranded
stylish
submit
substitute
sue
supervise
surrounding
suspended

technology
temporary
terminal
tracking
transfer
transmission
tread

underage
uninsured
unrestricted
updated
upkeep

valid
vandalism
violation
vision

warranty
wholesale
willful
wobble
workmanship

yield
zero tolerance

Index

Index

Index